DATE DUE

956.95
Jor   Jordan

Children of the World

Jordan

For their help in the preparation of *Children of the World: Jordan*, the editors gratefully thank Employment and Immigration Canada, Ottawa, Ont.; the US Immigration and Naturalization Service, Washington, DC; the Embassy of Jordan (US), Washington, DC; the International Institute of Wisconsin, Milwaukee; the United States Department of State, Bureau of Public Affairs, Office of Public Communication, Washington, DC, for unencumbered use of material in the public domain; and Basel Said, Milwaukee.

Library of Congress Cataloging-in-Publication Data

Jordan.

(Children of the world)
"Originally published in shortened
form consisting of section I only"—
"First and originally published by Kaisei-sha Publishing Co., Ltd., Tokyo"—
Bibliography: p.
Includes index.
 Summary: Presents the life of a Bedouin-Palestinian boy and his family living in Amman, Jordan, describing his home, school, daily activities, and some of the traditions and celebrations of his country.
1. Jordan—Juvenile literature. 2. Children—Jordan—
Juvenile literature. 3. Jordan—Social life and customs—
Juvenile literature. 4. Family life—Jordan—Juvenile
literature. [1. Jordan—Social life and customs.
2. Family life—Jordan] I. Hirokawa Ryuichi, 1943-
II. Wright, David K. III. Knowlton, MaryLee, 1946-
IV. Series: Children of the world (Milwaukee, Wis.)
DS153.J663 1988   956.95   87-42618
ISBN 1-55532-249-2
ISBN 1-55532-224-7 (lib. bdg.)

North American edition first published in 1988 by

Gareth Stevens, Inc.
7317 West Green Tree Road   Milwaukee, Wisconsin 53223, USA

This work was originally published in shortened form consisting of section I only.
Photographs and original text copyright © 1987 by Hirokawa Ryuichi.
First and originally published by Kaisei-sha Publishing Co., Ltd., Tokyo.
World English rights arranged with Kaisei-sha Publishing Co., Ltd. through
Japan Foreign-Rights Centre.

Copyright this format © 1988 by Gareth Stevens, Inc.
Additional material and maps copyright © 1988 by Gareth Stevens, Inc.

Typeset by Ries Graphics ltd., Milwaukee.
Design: Laurie Bishop and Laurie Shock.
Map design: Gary Moseley.

1   2   3   4   5   6   7   8   9   92   91   90   89   88

Children of the World
Jordan

Photography by
Hirokawa Ryuichi

Edited by
David K. Wright &
MaryLee Knowlton

Gareth Stevens Publishing
Milwaukee

. . . a note about *Children of the World*:

The children of the world live in fishing towns, Arctic regions, and urban centers, on islands and in mountain valleys, on sheep ranches and fruit farms. This series follows one child in each country through the pattern of his or her life. Candid photographs show the children with their families, at school, at play, and in their communities. The text describes the dreams of the children and, often through their own words, tells how they see themselves and their lives.

Each book also explores events that are unique to the country in which the child lives, including festivals, religious ceremonies, and national holidays. The *Children of the World* series does more than tell about foreign countries. It introduces the child of each country and shows readers what it is like to be a child in that country.

. . . and about *Jordan*:

Ali Habashne, a boy of Bedouin and Palestinian descent, lives in Amman, the capital of Jordan. Jordan is a country with both a rich cultural heritage and a vital role in complex and troubling world events. Ali's story includes an account of a trip he takes to places of great historical and personal interest.

To enhance this book's value in libraries and classrooms, comprehensive reference sections include up-to-date data about Jordan's geography, demographics, language, currency, education, culture, industry, and natural resources. *Jordan* also features a bibliography, research topics, activity projects, and discussions of such subjects as Amman, the country's history, political system, ethnic and religious composition, and language.

The living conditions and experiences of children in Jordan vary tremendously according to economic, environmental, and ethnic circumstances. The reference sections help bring to life for young readers the diversity and richness of the culture and heritage of Jordan. Of particular interest are discussions of the cultures and national groups that have made their presence felt in Jordan today — especially the Palestinians, Jordan's largest single national group and a people that have helped place Jordan squarely in the center politically as well as geographically of the world's most volatile and fascinating region.

CONTENTS

Ali's family: his father, Mustahfa; Ali; his mother, Hadeja; and his brother, Anmahl.

LIVING IN JORDAN:
Ali, a Boy with an Ancient Heritage

Ali Habashne is eight years old. He lives in the capital of Jordan, Amman, a city of about one million people. His family includes his father, Mustahfa; his mother, Hadeja; and his older brother, Anmahl, who is 12. Jordan is mostly ridges, hills, and desert. It is in the area of the world known as the Middle East.

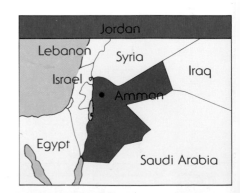

6

Ali lives in this apartment building.

Ali and his mother leave the apartment.

Downtown Amman.

A Small and Busy Family

Ali's first name means "outstanding person" in Arabic, his language. The most famous person named Ali in Middle East history became a hero. He died defending Islam, the religion of most Jordanians.

The family eats lunch together.

Ali shops with his father.

Ali's mother takes him to the Children's Club, a place with things for young people to do.

Ali's father's name, Mustahfa, is another version of the name Mohammed. Mohammed founded the Islamic religion. Hadeja, Ali's mother's name, means "delicate." Anmahl means "city builder." Ali's family is smaller than the families in which his parents grew up. That is because people who live in Amman usually have smaller families than people in rural areas. Ali likes the special attention he gets from being in a small family.

Mustahfa works in an office in downtown Amman. Hadeja takes care of the family and recently began taking college classes once again. Ali and Anmahl go to school. The family eats together at noon and in the evening. A Jordanian meal can include rice with vegetables and mutton, which is meat from a sheep.

Ali brushes his teeth before bed.

Supper in the living room.

Ali gets up early, usually at 5:30 a.m. He leaves for school at 6:15 and returns home at 2:00 p.m. By then, his father is home and the family has lunch together. His father then returns to his office. Between lunch and supper, Ali plays or visits friends. Three times a week, he goes to the Children's Club for games and activities.

At home or at the home of his friend, Gais, Ali likes to watch television. Shows from Europe, North America, and Japan carry subtitles in Arabic. Among the most popular shows for children are karate cartoons. Ali especially likes Japanese stories featuring Ninjas, which are karate warriors.

Ali at the home of a friend, Gais.

Ali and Gais practice karate.

In the evening, Ali does homework, plays with Anmahl, or watches TV. He and Anmahl often disagree over which shows to watch. Their father says they are like cartoon characters — always fighting or chasing each other.

Ali enjoys coloring.

A nightly chore: getting ready for school.

Bedtime for Ali is 9:00 p.m. Just before bed, he lays out tomorrow's clothes and makes sure his homework is done. As he drifts off to sleep, he dreams of teaching karate.

Ali plays a game of skill on the TV set.

Ali's father is in the movie and video business. He brings television programs into Jordan from other countries. He's pleased he is able to bring in the right kinds of shows for Ali and other children of his country.

Ali plays in his father's office.

Ali's father is from Palestine. For centuries, Palestine had been ruled by many outsiders, including the Greeks, Romans, and British. The people who lived in Palestine included Jews and Arabs alike. After World War II, many Jews fled Europe for Palestine. In 1948, parts of Palestine became the Jewish state of Israel. Today, many Palestinians live in Jordan and elsewhere. Some, like Ali's father, have become citizens of other countries. Others live in refugee camps or fight the Israelis from secret bases in the Middle East. Most Palestinians want a homeland of their own.

He deposits his allowance in a bank.

Ali runs to catch the school bus.

Ali's principal is a man named Dawake.

Students line up to enter school.

Getting off the bus at home.

Ali's School

Ali catches the school bus without eating breakfast. His mother packs him a sandwich which he eats with his classmates each day at the 10:00 a.m. recess. There are 30 students in Ali's 3rd grade class, which is in a private school named Al Raed Alarabi.

Children play soccer during gym class.

Ali's school is just over a large hill from his home. His parents chose to send their son to a private school because private schools in Jordan are said to have better facilities and better teachers. Ali attends a full day, six days a week. Public schools have half-day classes.

Ali's school has 500 students. The youngest children go to kindergarten. Children 6-12 attend elementary school, while children 13-15 go to junior high school.

Arabic language class.

Five classes meet each day. Each class meets for 50 minutes, with a five-minute break in between. In mostly Muslim schools such as this one, there is no school on Friday, the religious holiday. Christian schools are not in session on Sunday. Ali and his friends get a summer vacation from the end of June to the end of August and have a vacation at the end of Ramadan, a holy month. Ramadan usually ends in September.

Children enjoy art class.

Ali studies Arabic, English, arithmetic, science, history, religion, art, and physical education. His favorite subjects are religion and physical education.

Tumbling during gym class.

Ali's report card. His grades are good!

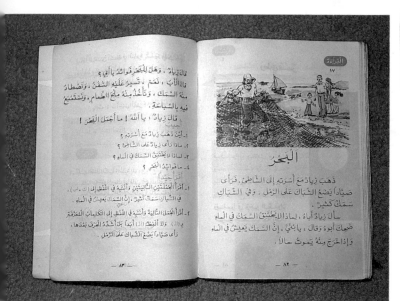

An Arabic textbook.

Ali's school bag.

What does Ali want to be when he grows up? He thinks for a while with his arms folded and a dreamy look on his face. Ali wants to be a karate teacher. His teacher tells him he's too young to worry about his future. Ali agrees. He certainly does not appear to worry much, in school or at home!

Jordanians — A History of Learning

Education is important to Jordanians. They are among the best educated in their part of the world. Six years of elementary school and three years of junior high school are required. After that come three years of high school, which are optional.

Ali's fellow students.

Papercutting crafts at the Children's Club. Ali goes to the club three times a week.

A picture drawn by Ali.

Ali and his fellow students don't always take school seriously. But their ancestors were some of the greatest scholars of all time. Arabs were pioneers in medicine, astronomy, and mathematics. Drawings of how to perform surgery appear on ancient Arab scrolls. They are still very accurate and easy to follow.

Jordanians often use their education to make money outside the country and bring it home. At present, about 300,000 well-educated Jordanians work in Europe, Africa, and other parts of the Middle East. These Jordanians are mostly business people, engineers, scientists, and teachers.

Palestinians, too, pride themselves on their education. So being in a refugee camp without a job or a chance to show their skills is very hard. No matter how well they are treated, refugees live on the edge of society.

Refugees and Jordanians alike recall their glorious past. Many believe the Middle East has a bright future. Adults work hard for the future. That is why Ali attends the Children's Club: so his parents can work. They know he is well taken care of there.

The Children's Club playground.

Ali loves to read books.

The children draw pictures of clowns.

A photo studio.

A general store.

Visiting the Market

Amman's many neighborhoods are separated by hills called *jabals.* Ali's house is on one of these hills. East of his house in a valley is downtown, with its many shops. The collection of shops and sellers is called the *souk,* or market.

A great variety of items can be found in Amman's market. Fresh and canned fruits or vegetables, carry-out foods, television sets, tailors' shops, butcher shops, and more are around every corner. The shops are open from early morning to late at night.

24

A store selling mutton.

The market is a noisy place. Ali hears the clatter of glasses from the water seller, the whinny of horses, and the voice of a vendor shouting prices: "One lira, one lira!" He finds it all very exciting.

Five times a day, the voice of the *muezzin*, or priest, booms through the market, calling Muslims to prayer. "Allah is great," calls the priest. This reminds believers in Islam that it is time to bow toward the holy city of Mecca and to say prayers.

Schawarma, a beef-and-lamb sandwich, is a favorite.

A used-clothing dealer.

The souk in Amman.

A shop selling grains and spices.

Many tourists walk about the souk because it is a busy, fun place. They come to Amman to see many other sights as well. They come to see an ancient coliseum built by the Romans and to look at the famous Fusem Mosque and other sites. Ali likes the ancient buildings. But he is more interested in the tasty foods and other items sold in the souk.

This dessert, called a *harisa*, is baked in an oven. It's made of flour, eggs, sugar, yogurt, baking powder, pine nuts, and syrup. Slices are sold to shoppers.

A Homecoming

One day, Ali goes with his mother to visit Karak, her hometown. She takes him because he is interested in the history of her side of his family.

That history is a long one. Her family once were nomads, moving their livestock from one watering hole to another. They came to Jordan with fellow Muslims in the 7th century A D. The family settled in the village of Karak and fought the Christian crusaders.

The crusaders came from Europe to take the Holy Land away from Muslims in the years 1096-1291.

Not long ago, Ali's mother visited a dentist. When the dentist found out who her family was, he would not take payment for fixing her teeth. He said her family had saved his ancestors, who were Christians from Karak.

Ali and his mother leave about 7:00 a.m. They drive out of Amman by car. There are two ways to get to Karak. A new highway, called Desert Road, is quick. But the travelers choose the old King's Road because it goes through more towns and villages. King's Road is so named because soldiers sent by different kings have used it for thousands of years.

Ali and Hadeja's destination: the village of Karak.

A shepherd retrieves a lamb that has fallen from a truck.

After six hours, Ali and Hadeja arrive in Rakin, where two of Hadeja's aunts live. This is Hadeja's first visit in 20 years, and she is happy to see that many of the old ways still remain.

Farmers use horses to plow.

Many telephone calls are made to announce her arrival! Relatives from all over the village come to see her. Ali's mother tells him that here and in Karak, where she was born, he can trace his family lines back over hundreds of years.

Ali's mother loves the many old-fashioned village customs. They can be seen on any street. For example, yogurt is made in a sheepskin bag. And water is pulled up by hand from the village well.

Today a wedding is taking place. The men do all the cooking for the special event. They cook lamb in a big pot and put the cooked lamb's head in the middle of a big plate of rice. Everyone in the village attends the wedding, which ends after the dinner. Ali loves the big ceremony.

Relatives gather for a reunion.

Ali strums a guitar.

Here is where the wedding takes place.

Milk is turned into yogurt in a sheepskin bag.

Street stalls sell everything.

Ali Explores Karak

From Rakin, Ali and his mother take a bus to Karak. Karak is about 1,500 years old and sits atop a hill. On one side of the town is the castle built by crusaders. Ali was a little boy when he last visited Karak. Everything seems new to him.

He loves exploring underground passages in the old castle. He enjoys the castle museum, where he sees pictures of fish painted on ancient pottery.

In a candy store.

Buildings in Karak are usually two stories high. Here and there, ancient building walls can still be seen. Ali's mother takes him to one of the old buildings. "This is the house where I was born," she tells him.

Eating mutton from a big plate.

34

Later, as Ali and his mother are walking down a village street, something strange happens. People Ali has never seen come up to them and warmly shake hands. "Who are these people?" Ali wonders. His mother explains that many of the people who live on the street are their relatives. They, too, are named Habashne and have the same ancestors as Ali. He realizes that he is part of an ancient family.

Ali is not sure he understands exactly how he is related to these people. But he decides not to worry about it and has a nice time. He sleeps the way many villagers sleep — on a mattress on the floor.

Some crops can be grown in the desert.

Baking bread in a Bedouin tent.

Meeting the Bedouins

From Karak, Ali and his mother take a bus to the historic Dead Sea, which is really a salty lake formed by the Jordan River. Along the way, they see many people living in tents. These people are called Bedouins. They lead a nomadic life in the desert. Ali's mother asks about a relative who might be living in one of the tents. She is told that the relative moved just two days before Ali and his mother arrived.

Some plants grow in the desert.

At play in the desert.

A pepper.

An edible desert plant.

Bedouins live very close to nature. They can predict the weather and are well prepared to catch precious rain when it falls. Some modern Bedouins carry passports so they can move back and forth between Jordan and neighboring countries.

The house of Ali's great-grandmother, who lives near the Dead Sea.

Olives.

Too much movement by the Bedouins can cause problems, the government believes. Recently, officials told the Bedouins that they can no longer move wherever they like. Are they as happy now as they were when they could move all over? Ali wonders.

Only thorny shrubs grow along the road to the Dead Sea. Hadeja says her great-grandmother and her great-grandmother's oldest sons moved near the Dead Sea to farm because the winters are very mild. Ali wonders how you can farm where only thorns grow.

But to his surprise, he finds green and healthy plants growing in the Jordan Valley, far below sea level. Truckloads of freshly harvested tomatoes are being shipped out of the area as Ali and his mother near great-grandmother's home.

Ali's mother tells him that this is one of the first areas where farming took place — 10,000 years ago. The farmers cannot use water from the Dead Sea because the salt would kill the crops. So they get water from mountain streams. Because of the warm climate, some crops can be grown and picked twice a year.

At his great-grandmother's farm, Ali joins some Bedouin children who are running after sheep, donkeys, and camels. Since it is spring, many animals have just had babies.

Ali shares a comic book with his cousins.

Yogurt mixed with herbs.

Breakfast at his great-grandmother's house.

Bread dipped in olive oil.

The Dead Sea shoreline is red.

The salt helps swimmers float with ease!

The Dead Sea and Petra

The Dead Sea is a 10-minute ride from the home of Ali's great-grandmother. The shore of the sea is the lowest point on Earth — 1,300 feet (396.5 m) below sea level. Because so much salt has dissolved in the water, swimmers do not sink, and no fish or animal can live here. Ali remembers once getting salt water in his eyes, and he decides not to go in.

Mother and son return to the King's Road. From there, they take the eight-hour ride to the historic ruins at Petra. The last 40 minutes of the trip will be on foot.

On the way to Petra.

This marker is 1,300 feet (396.5 m) above the Dead Sea.

SEA LEVEL

The entrance to Petra is a treasure house more than 2,100 years old.

The fortress-like town of Petra was built by the Nabatia people. They came from the desert about 2,500 years ago, in the 6th century B.C.

Part of an ancient coliseum.

Petra: Ali's view of the huge stone ruins as he comes upon them on foot.
The pink stone is called nubia.

The moon rises over Amman, Ali's home town.

Amman — Home Again

Amman looks different to Ali, now that he has seen some of Jordan's historic sights. Ali loved seeing the Bedouins, his other relatives, the Dead Sea, and Petra. But he says he likes living in Amman best.

He enjoys Amman because it has modern conveniences. He also likes the toy stores, visiting his father's office, playing at the Children's Club, and his many school friends. Like children in other parts of the world, he prefers the faster pace of city life to the leisure and natural beauty of the country.

This modern building houses a bank, a supermarket, and theaters.

The main street in downtown Amman.

A busy newsstand.

Relatives on Ali's mother's side living in Amman.

Ali's maternal grandfather.

Ali's newborn cousin.

More Relatives!

Asuma, Ali's aunt and his father's sister, has given birth to a baby. Ali joins his relatives to celebrate. Everyone agrees on Mortase as the baby's name. The name means "a special way to take care of important things." Everyone enjoys being with each other at this happy time.

Ali looks at his family and is proud of his Palestinian and Bedouin heritage. Although about half of Jordan's population is Palestinian, Ali understands that many Palestinians are without a country. He hopes he will grow up to be someone who helps build a peaceful world.

Relatives on Ali's father's side living in Amman.

FOR YOUR INFORMATION: Jordan

Official name: Hashemite Kingdom of Jordan
al Mamlaka al Urduniya al Hashemiyah
(al mahm-LAH-kah al ur-doo-NEE-ah al hah-shem-EE-yah)

Capital: Amman

History

Jordan — A Middle East Crossroads

Before there were Jordanians, there was the land we now call Jordan. The first settlers arrived about 2000 BC. They made homes in fertile areas on the banks of the Jordan River at a place called Canaan.

These people were highly civilized. For centuries, they had been creating large buildings and art that can still be seen today. The tribe of settlers was called Amorites. Down through the centuries, their small land was invaded by many other people. Egyptians, Israelites, Persians, Greeks, Romans, and Turks are just a few of the nations that ruled the Jordan riverbanks.

Coliseum in Amman. It was built when the Romans ruled the country.

No other country on Earth has been invaded more often. That is because Jordan is near busy pathways connecting Africa, Asia, and Europe. It is close to the east end of the Mediterranean Sea and has a port city on the Red Sea. Conquerors gathered supplies for trips across the sea or across the desert in Jordan's small but fertile growing area.

The Importance of Religion

Because so many people came to Jordan, natives were exposed to many religions. But today three-fourths of the people follow Islam. This religion began in the Arabian desert about 600 AD. It spread through Jordan, where most desert wanderers, farmers, shepherds, and villagers became believers. Islam has been the most important influence on people who live in Jordan to this day. Its followers are called Muslims.

One-quarter of the people living in Jordan are Christians. They trace their religious roots to the very first Christians from nearby Israel. Other Christians arrived in the 11th, 12th, and 13th centuries. They were European crusaders who wanted to win back Christian holy lands from the Muslims.

These Christian knights fought fierce battles that killed many people and converted few. During one crusade, thousands of small children were sent from Europe to fight. Many died or were killed along the trail to what is now Jordan.

The Turkish empire ruled Jordan from 1500 AD until the 20th century. One of its major accomplishments was to run a railroad through Jordan for Islamic religious travelers. The railroad was blown up during World War I by a British adventurer who called himself Lawrence of Arabia.

Modern Boundaries Are Formed

At about the same time, a man from the Hashemite Arab tribe named Sharif Hussein led a revolt against the Turks. He was from the religious city of Mecca, and he rallied people in the area by appealing to their Arab heritage.

The Turks were overthrown and, in 1923, the independent Emirate of Transjordan was established. *Emirate* means *state*. The new land was created from what had been a corner of Arabia. It existed under British protection and was ruled by the son of Sharif Hussein, King Emir Abdullah.

The British were governing land near Jordan that included parts of Palestine that are known today as Israel, Gaza, and the city of Jerusalem. This entire area became an important meeting place during World War II for the British and their allies. In 1946, British rule ended and the Emirate of Transjordan became the independent Hashemite Kingdom of Transjordan. Two years later, British rule over Palestine ended and the state of Israel was founded on land the Palestinians said belonged to them. Fighting began.

Many Israelis were European Jews who had barely escaped death at the hands of the Germans or Russians during World War II. They decided to defend the new land at all costs. The Palestinians turned to Arab neighbors, including Transjordan, for help. A truce signed in 1949 gave Transjordan the land west of the Jordan River, the area now known as the West Bank. The anger continued.

That anger showed on July 20, 1951, when King Abdullah was shot to death on the steps of a mosque, an Islamic church, where he had gone to pray. His son, Prince Talal, was named king. But he was a weak ruler and the throne was passed in 1952 to Talal's son, Al Hussein ibn Talal. King Hussein was only 18 years of age, but he had been taught a great deal by his grandfather.

Hussein Takes the Throne

King Hussein went to elementary school in Jordan, where he and his family lived in a five-room home instead of a palace. He attended school in Egypt before being sent to a famous military school in England. He was with his grandfather when the old king was shot. A second bullet, aimed at Hussein, bounced off a medal he was wearing, and he escaped injury.

The king has ruled his country for more than 35 years. It has not always been easy. Jordan has served as a home for many Palestinians. Are they refugees or should they try to settle in Jordan, since Israel now claims the land Palestinians view as their homeland?

Mistrust between Arabs and Israelis grew until it erupted in 1967 in the Six-Day War. Jordan joined Syria, Egypt, and Iraq against Israel. The Israelis, with better training and equipment, won the war and took over the West Bank of the Jordan River. *Fedayeen*, Palestinian refugees who want to continue the fight, have conducted raids into Israel. In 1970, they fought a brief war with Jordan, and in 1971, despite support from Syria, the fedayeen were chased out of Jordan.

This action has made some Arabs — and most Palestinians — suspicious of King Hussein. For years, the king has walked a careful line between Israel and his Arab friends. He has also managed to increase the wealth of his country, even though it is almost 90 percent desert or rocky hills.

King Hussein and Modern Jordan

King Hussein is married to Queen Noor, an American from California. They have six children. He loves flying, fishing, playing soccer and rugby, and driving fast cars and motorcycles. Most Jordanians respect the king. Many people see him as an important person in the search for peace in the Middle East.

Jordan has few natural resources. Yet its economy has grown rapidly under King Hussein. Irrigation has improved crop yields along the Jordan River, while potash

50

fertilizer is mined near the Dead Sea. The 1967 war meant the loss of the rich West Bank, and this loss created unemployment for thousands of Palestinians. But five years later, the country was back on its feet. Today, Jordan manufactures such items as cement and prescription drugs and has built many schools and hospitals.

Language

No one speaks Classic Arabic, the tongue heard five times a day as a priest calls Muslims to worship. But the various dialects are rich and pleasant to hear. English is the foreign language most often taught in schools.

Sometimes, a Jordanian's dialect will tell what part of the country he or she is from. Most residents are Arabs who trace their ancestors from ancient tribes who lived north or south of modern Jordan. Some believe their ancestors to be related to the founder of the Islamic religion, Mohammed. Their family trees have been passed down to them in writing and in songs and poems.

Education

Schooling is important to Jordanians, who go six years to elementary school and three years to junior high. After that, students can receive either general or special training for a specific job. There are three types of schools: public, private, and religious. Two colleges have a total of 27,000 students, and a military and police college has 400 students. There is also a medical school.

Jordanian public schools are almost free. Parents pay a small sum each year for their children to attend. Private schools are quite expensive. A year in a Muslim or Christian school costs about $1,000 in Amman. In both public and private schools, books must be purchased by students. There are enough public schools for all students, but public schools are not as good as private schools, most parents believe. How can you tell if a child goes to private school? He or she will be wearing a uniform.

As in North America, the job of teaching is a respected position. But teaching does not pay very well. Many private school teachers cannot afford to send their own children to a private school. Private and public schools alike are in session year round. There are four months of study, a month of exams, and a month of vacation, twice a year. Vacations are based on religious holidays. In some schools, vacations are given for Muslim and for Christian holidays, even though the school is all Muslim.

Many high school graduates want to go to college. But there are not nearly enough colleges. The University of Jordan in Amman is the country's best university. It has a beautiful campus and many foreign students. Those who cannot afford the university but want more education often go to trade schools.

Population and Ethnic Groups

About 2.7 million Jordanians have made their home on the East Bank. They barely outnumber Palestinian refugees. One million people live in the capital city, Amman. Arabic is their language, but English is spoken in the cities. About 70 percent of the people live in urban areas. This is likely to increase as rural residents continue to move to the cities. The West Bank population changes overnight. Right now, around 800,000 Jordanians live there.

The majority of non-Arabs who are Jordanian citizens are Armenians. These Christians were all but wiped out by Turks during World War I. Their country, Armenia, is now a part of the Soviet Union. Others who used to live in the Soviet Union include Muslim Circassians from near the Caucasus Mountains. There are also very small communities of ancient Jewish groups, plus Greeks, Turks, and others.

Palestinians make up the largest minority, but the Bedouins are among the most interesting. These desert people, famed for their fighting ability, poetry, and hospitality, number fewer than 50,000 in Jordan. They live in tribes. Some are seminomadic, which means they have no permanent homes but move where their animals can find food and where there is water.

Women in traditional dress.

Some Bedouin women wear very beautiful, very ornate costumes. An experienced person can tell where a Bedouin woman lives by the type of long dress she wears. Jewels, coins, beads, and geometric designs adorn the dresses, which can be yards long when unwrapped.

Government

Jordan is a new country with an old form of government. It is ruled by a king. But the people also have a constitution that protects them and that they obey. Each king inherits the crown from his father and then must obey the constitution, too. The king is in charge of all branches of government. He works with judges and with an upper house of parliament that he appoints. There are no political parties, but males over 18 can cast votes in elections for the lower of the two houses of parliament. The king is also commander in chief of the armed forces.

The country is divided into eight political areas. Each area is run by a man picked by the minister of the interior. Cities and villages have mayors and elected councils. The West Bank is occupied by Israeli forces but has village officials, just like the rest of Jordan.

There are three kinds of courts. One kind interprets the laws of the country. Another kind is for religious matters. The third kind is for questions concerning land and other possessions.

Jordan's government raises money by taxing its people. The government uses the money to support an army and to build schools, hospitals, roads, and houses. Housing is especially needed for the two million Palestinians on the Jordan River's East Bank.

King Hussein prides himself on being a diplomat. He has tried at different times to bring Arabs and Israelis to the bargaining table. The United States supports Israel but supplies weapons to both Jordan and Israel.

Climate

The country has a dry climate with hot, sunny days and cool nights. The temperature in Amman averages 73°F (23°C) from May to October and 55°F (13°C) from November to April. Temperatures can go above 100°F (122°C) for days in the desert, where annual rainfall is about four inches (10 cm) or less.

The area near the Dead Sea can be intensely hot, with some unusual weather. Hot weather causes fast evaporation, and that makes a haze over the sea — even on cloudless days. The evaporation leaves salt, which mixes with the incoming water from the River Jordan and keeps the sea salty. The salt also helps keep swimmers afloat. In fact, the water is so salty and heavy that a floating person seems to be lying directly on top of the water.

Land

Jordan is 37,737 sq miles (97,740 sq km) in area. This makes it about the size of the state of Maine. Its neighbors include Israel on the west, Syria on the north, Iraq on the east, and Saudi Arabia on the south.

Jordan has deserts, hills, plains, mountains, a few forests, and even a tiny sea coast at the south end of the country. It is mainly a high plateau divided by valleys and gorges. Although it is usually warm, snow can be seen on higher peaks. There are a few oases. These are spots where there is fresh water for humans and animals as well as for trees and plants. Jordan has irrigated some areas, adding a lot to crop yields.

A huge crack in the earth, called a rift, runs from north to south. The Jordan River has taken this as its path. The river empties into the Dead Sea, which is 1,302 feet (400m) below seal level. That is the lowest point on earth. The Dead Sea is so named because it has so much salt. A fish swimming into the sea from the river dies instantly. Only certain bacteria can live in the water.

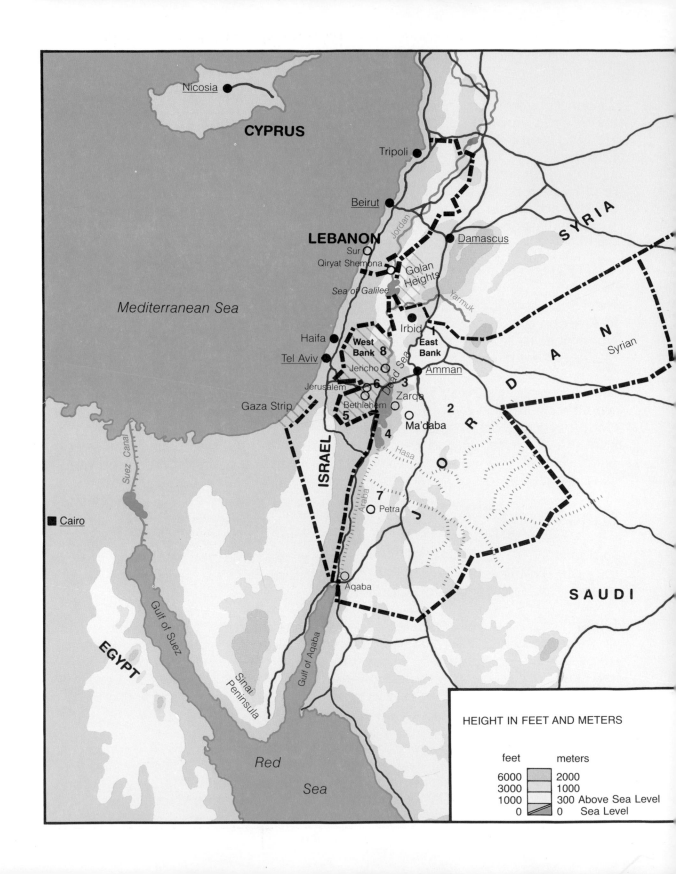

HEIGHT IN FEET AND METERS

feet	meters	
6000	2000	
3000	1000	
1000	300	Above Sea Level
0	0	Sea Level

JORDAN - Political and Physical

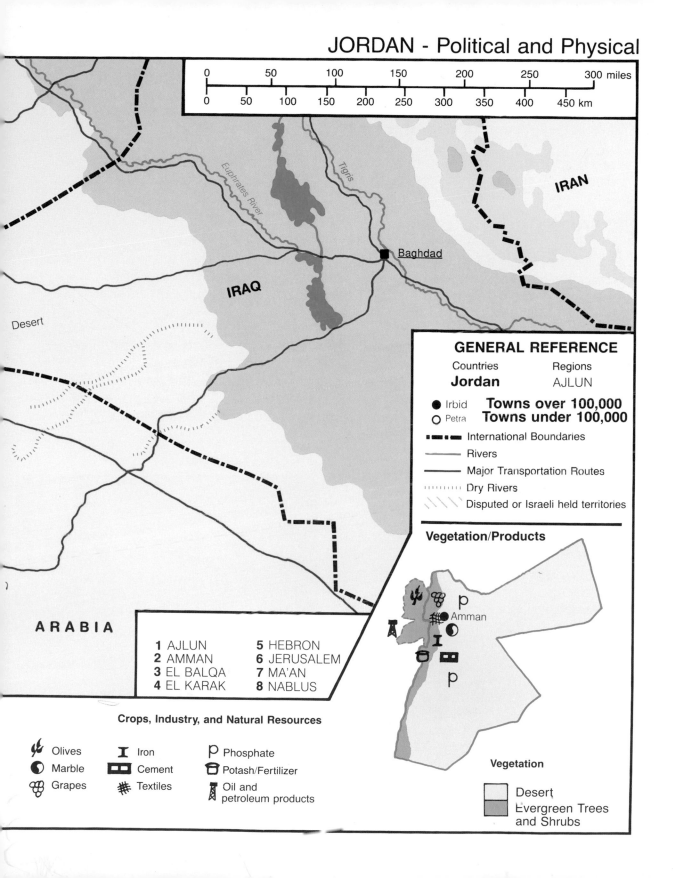

| 0 | 50 | 100 | 150 | 200 | 250 | 300 miles |
| 0 | 50 | 100 | 150 | 200 | 250 | 300 | 350 | 400 | 450 km |

Euphrates River

Tigris

IRAN

Baghdad

IRAQ

Desert

ARABIA

GENERAL REFERENCE

Countries	Regions
Jordan	AJLUN

● Irbid **Towns over 100,000**
○ Petra **Towns under 100,000**

▬▪▬ International Boundaries
— Rivers
— Major Transportation Routes
·········· Dry Rivers
/////// Disputed or Israeli held territories

Vegetation/Products

Amman

1 AJLUN
2 AMMAN
3 EL BALQA
4 EL KARAK
5 HEBRON
6 JERUSALEM
7 MA'AN
8 NABLUS

Crops, Industry, and Natural Resources

🕊 Olives
◐ Marble
🍇 Grapes
I Iron
▭▭ Cement
✳ Textiles
P Phosphate
▯ Potash/Fertilizer
🛢 Oil and petroleum products

Vegetation

Desert
Evergreen Trees and Shrubs

Natural Resources

Jordan mines thousands of tons of phosphates and potash, which are minerals used in fertilizer. Other minerals commonly found include gypsum, limestone, kaolin, glass sands, marble, granite, and feldspar. Explorers are seeking copper, uranium, and oil, but they have made no major discoveries.

There are hardly any forests in Jordan, since rainfall is scant. One source of water has been created by dams, which also provide the country with electricity and irrigation.

Agriculture and Industry

Farming is closely related to the water supply. In recent years, the government has helped farmers increase the number of acres used for crops. Jordanians grow enough to meet their needs. They import many luxury items, but imports are balanced by a number of exports.

Major industries include fertilizer, cement, petroleum (oil) products, electricity, iron, cloth, medicine, paper, and leather. The variety of products shows how skilled modern Jordanians are. To encourage investment by foreigners, the country has created several free-trade zones. At these sites, there are no taxes and no rentals charged on buildings. Combined with laws that encourage investment money, the free-trade zones have been quite a success.

More and more people are providing services as Jordanians earn more income. Hundreds of doctors and nurses are trained in Jordan, in Europe, and in North America each year to staff 32 modern hospitals. Because of the fighting in Lebanon, many Middle Easterners now view Jordan as the best place to go in the Arab Middle East for medical attention, shopping, and travel.

A shepherd near Jerash.

Jordan is also becoming known for its modern communications system. In addition to color television transmission by satellite from the United States and Europe, Jordanians have modern telephone and postal service. The country has three daily newspapers printed in Arabic and one printed in English.

Sports

Many of the sports played in Jordan reflect King Hussein's British education. Soccer is immensely popular, and there are world-class players throughout the Middle East.

There is a government-backed water festival each year in Aqaba that features such sports as sailing and windsurfing.

On the outskirts of Amman is Hussein Sports City, a complex for the country's most popular sport, soccer. The complex also has track and field areas, tennis and basketball courts, swimming pools, large gardens, and spectator areas that seat more than 25,000 fans.

Motorsports, involving cars and cycles, have become popular since major roads have been paved and improved. At least one international car rally is held in Jordan each year.

Religion

It is sometimes hard for non-Muslims to imagine how important religion is in a Muslim's daily life. Ninety percent of all Jordanians are of the Sunni branch of Islam. That means almost everyone's most deeply held beliefs are the same.

Islam was founded in Arabia in the 7th century AD by Mohammed. He told followers that God (*Allah* in Arabic) is the only God and that they must strictly follow him. Mohammed's teachings are gathered in the Koran, a book that is sacred to all Muslims. They believe the Koran to be the word of God, given to Mohammed by the angel Gabriel.

The religion spread from the desert as far west as Europe and as far east as Southeast Asia and the Pacific islands. Conquering Muslim armies forced prisoners to convert to Islam or pay taxes for the cost of their protection. But a more important reason for its triumph over other religions was its simplicity. A person is considered a Muslim if he or she follows the Five Pillars of Faith:

1. The profession of faith. Every Muslim must say the following aloud once in his or her lifetime: "There is no God but Allah, and Mohammed is his Prophet."

2. Prayer. A believer must pray five times daily, in a mosque if one is near.

3. The *zakat* (tax). This must be paid once a year on most possessions. It is to be given to or spent on the poor.

4. Fasting. Muslims should not eat in daylight hours for one entire month each year. This holy month is called Ramadan.

5. The *hajj* (pilgrimage). Every Muslim is expected to make a religious trip to the holy city of Mecca, Saudi Arabia, once or twice in his or her life, if possible.

Islam affects everyday life of most Muslims. Friday is their sabbath, so on that day public offices and many shops are closed. Islam influences the banking system, laws, courts, schools, clothing, food, and behavior toward members of the opposite sex and nonbelievers.

A deeply religious Muslim finds Islam to be a great comfort. The Koran can provide an answer wherever there are questions about morality, personal behavior, or any other kind of right versus wrong. But there are disadvantages. Men and women have different rights under the Koran. Some Muslims also believe that the results of progress may break rules of the Koran. In modern Jordan, where education and hard work make up for a lack of natural resources, choosing between the Koran and current ideas is hard for many Muslims.

Today's Jordanians want to keep religion and culture free from the influence of the Soviet Union and Western countries. The Soviets are seen as godless and are not trusted since they invaded Afghanistan. Jordanians also are worried about the greed and immorality they think seeps into their society from the United States. Such feelings have helped the cause of Muslim conservatives. Some conservatives also view Israel as an enemy of the Islamic faith.

Several small Christian sects have for centuries existed peacefully. So have Shiite Muslims, followers of Islam whose beliefs have differed since ancient times with those of the majority Sunnis.

Arts and Crafts

Classic Art and Architecture

Jordanians today produce a variety of wonderful crafts. Visitors and residents buy jewelry, rugs, leather goods, pottery, glass, wood and metalwork, straw work, and basketry. The historical art and architecture from this part of the world is even more magnificent. And much of it can still be seen in Jordan.

This classic art also includes literature, dance, and music. It is tied to the Islamic religion. Unlike Western art, which usually has a beginning, a middle, and an end, Islamic art has no such goals. Instead, its patterns seem to come from nowhere and go on forever. Experts say this shows the belief among Muslims that only God can create beginnings and endings.

Typical of the great buildings created by Islamic artists are the mosques in the country. They are cool and clean, with a large, round roof over the hall where people pray. All mosques have towers, called minarets, that point like perfectly shaped spears into the sky. Before the age of loudspeakers, priests used the towers to call Muslims to prayer. Inside, mosaic art made of thousands of tiny stones will hold the viewer's eye. Such mosques are still used today in Amman and other large cities.

Petra and Iraq el Amir

Art, architecture, history, and tourism all come together in places such as Petra, a city carved out of pink rock by desert tribes long before there was an Islamic religion. The breathtaking city was built during the 2nd century BC. It was important for 600 years before being forgotten. Its rediscovery occurred in the 19th century when a canyon was being explored. Historians might conclude from looking at Petra that the Arab tribes were wonderful artists and builders who were simply waiting for a great religion to discover them!

There are even older sites, some dating from as early as the 8th century BC. Among them is Iraq el Amir, a ruin with early buildings and cave dwellings.

Jerusalem

All over Jordan there are fascinating blends of art, history, and religion. Perhaps the place best known by most Westerners is Jerusalem.

Three great religions, Christianity, Islam, and Judaism, meet in Jerusalem. All are represented by picturesque churches or mosques or temples. There are also ruins of great Roman buildings and aqueducts, which are long, wall-like devices built by ancient people to pipe water into the city. Everywhere a visitor turns in Jerusalem there is art — all of it ancient, much of it deeply religious.

Amman

This capital city is as old as the Bible and as new as today. It was a village in biblical times, named Philadelphia in honor of a Greek general. Amman was later inhabited by Romans, who built a huge outdoor theater. Arabs and Turks also ran the city until it became less important. King Abdullah picked Amman for his capital in the 1920s, and it has grown ever since.

Most of Jordan's major roads meet in Amman, which is also the home of a brand new airport. The airport serves as home base for Alia, the Royal Jordanian Airlines. This government-owned airline serves the Middle East, Europe, the United States, and Southeast Asia. Gigantic 747 aircraft can be seen every day over the capital.

There is no typical Amman resident. Women in expensive European clothes walk and talk with women wearing floor-length robes that have not changed for centuries. Men may wear suits or robes or even a combination of Western and Middle Eastern clothes. One side of the city has hotels, embassies, modern shops, and nice houses and apartments. In contrast, the opposite side of town is the site of refugee camps. This is the kind of problem Amman shares with many other world capitals — how to take care of its homeless.

Currency

The *dinar* and *fils* are the basic Jordanian currency. One dinar = 1,000 fils.

Jordanians in North America

Only about 600 Jordanians have emigrated to the United States during the last few years. An even smaller number has applied for Canadian citizenship. This is due to the fact that the country has a promising future, despite its being in the troubled Middle East.

As many as 300,000 Jordanians are out of their country at any one time. Many come to North America to study medicine, geology, and other sciences in colleges and universities. Many students from Jordan are Palestinians.

Like most people from the Middle East in North America, Jordanians tend to live in larger cities. Detroit is one US city popular with Middle Eastern immigrants.

Glossary of Useful Arabic Terms

abadan (ah-buh-DAHN) . . . . never
ah (ahk) . . . . brother
'alaikoom salam
   (ah-lay-KOOM sah-LAHM) . . . . . . Greetings (in reply to another's greeting)
am (um) . . . . mother
as-salam 'alaikoom
   (ah-sah-LAHM ah-lay-KOOM) . . . . Greetings (peace be with you)
at (aht) . . . . sister
daiman (die-MAHN) . . . . always
hajj (hodge) . . . . pilgrimage, religious trip
Kanesa (kuh-NAY-suh) . . . . Christian church
la (luh) . . . . no
ma (mah) . . . . water
ma alslama (mah ul-SLAH-muh) . . . goodbye
madrsa (muh-DRAH-suh) . . . . school
masjed (MAS-jeed) . . . . Mosque, Islamic church
marhapa (MAR-huh-puh) . . . . hello
medina (muh-DEEN-uh) . . . . city
muezzin (moo-EZZ-un) . . . . Muslim priest
na'am (nuh-AHM) . . . . yes
sahara (suh-HAR-uh) . . . . desert
souk (sook; rhymes with spook) . . . . market
waled (WAH-lud) . . . . father
shu biddak? (shoo bid-DAK) . . . . . . What do you want?
yimkin (YIM-kin) . . . . perhaps, maybe

More Books About Jordan

Here are some more books about Jordan. If you are interested in them, check your library. They may be helpful in doing research for the following "Things to Do" projects.

Bedouins. Peters (Silver Burdett)
I Am a Muslim. Aggarwal (Franklin Watts)
Legacy of the Desert: Understanding the Arabs. Archer (Little, Brown)

Things to Do — Research Projects

Many peoples and nations have lived in the land we know today as Jordan. For centuries, Jordan has truly been one of the world's great geographical and political crossroads. In our part of the 20th century, Jordan has again found itself at the crossroads of historic human events — this time, as an independent state playing a key role in one of the world's most turbulent trouble spots. Since the creation of Israel out of parts of Palestine in 1948, Jordan has been one of the region's major participants in the fighting between Arabs and Israelis. And today, it is one of the key participants in what may eventually become a Middle East peace process. As you read about Jordan, keep in mind the importance of current facts. Some of the research projects that follow need accurate, up-to-date information. That is why current newspapers and magazines are useful sources of information. Two publications your library may have will tell you about recent magazine and newspaper articles on many topics:

The Reader's Guide to Periodical Literature
Children's Magazine Guide

For accurate answers to questions about such topics of current interest as Jordan's relationship with its fellow Arab states, the Palestinians, and Israel, look up *Jordan* in these two publications. They will lead you to the most up-to-date information you can find.

1. How far is Amman, Jordan, from where you live? Using maps, travel guides, travel agents, or any other resources you know of, find out how you could get there and how long it would take.

2. Think of an occupation or career that interests you. Would you be able to do this kind of work in Jordan? Would being a male or female make a difference? Would your ethnic background make a difference? Use sources of recent information from the library for your information.

3. Find out the rights and responsibilities of a Muslim man or woman.

4. Look up *Jordan* in the *Reader's Guide to Periodical Literature* or the *Children's Magazine Guide.* Report to your classmates about what has been happening there in the past few months.

5. Religious wars have been very important in shaping Jordan and other countries in the Middle East. Using sources from the library, see how people of your religious persuasion have behaved in Jordan throughout its history.

More Things to Do - Activities

These projects should encourage you to think more about Jordan. They offer ideas for interesting group or individual projects you can do at school or home.

1. How does your life compare to Ali's? Write an imaginary letter to him. Explain how you are the same or different.

2. Why do you think it is important to study the history of Jordan today?

3. See if your town has any people who have come here from Jordan. Invite one or several to your class to talk about life in Jordan and their experiences in your country.

4. If you would like a pen pal in Jordan, write to these people:

International Pen Friends
P.O. Box 65
Brooklyn, New York 11229

Tell them your age and what country you want your pen pal to be from. Be sure to include your full name and address.

Index